The Three Reasons
You Don't Get Referrals

Frank Agin

The Three Reasons You Don't Get Referrals

Frank Agin
Founder & President
AmSpirit Business Connections

ISBN: 978-0-9823332-9-7

Published by:
418 Press, A Division of Four Eighteen Enterprises LLC
Post Office Box 30724, Columbus, Ohio 43230-0724

To my first networking partners!

Michael S. Agin
Carolyn Agin Bruno

Table of Contents

Introduction

"There are three reasons, and only three reasons, why you don't get referrals."

That's a statement that I've made at least a thousand times over the years.

- I've said it at various Chapter meetings (as well as individual members) of AmSpirit Business Connections.
- I've said it on countless Zoom calls with people and groups spanning the world.
- I've said it within programs I've delivered and speeches I've given.

I continue to say it because it's true. There are only three reasons why you don't get referrals.

I have come to this conclusion via working or talking with thousands of entrepreneurs, sales representatives, and professionals over the years. Many were involved with AmSpirit Business Connections. Some weren't in an organization at all but rather working with me on a consultative basis. Others were simply in a conversation with me – in person, on the phone, or over Zoom.

In each situation, they needed referrals but weren't getting them (or at least not the quality they wanted). And in each case the reason referrals were not happening always came down to one (or more) of the three reasons.

Here's The Reality

If you're trying to grow a business or build a clientele – and I assume that you are, because you're reading this – then you likely want referrals. Fair statement?

Referrals are great. In business, nothing can beat the notion of someone you know putting you in touch with someone you don't and saying, more or less:

"This is the person I was telling you about. They're good at what they do, and they will help you solve your problem."

- **Referrals!** They are far less expensive than advertising.

- **Referrals!** They are way better than a cold outreach to a total stranger.

- **Referrals!** They are far more effective than hoping a client just appears.

So, if referrals are what you're after, this is the book for you. In it, I'm going to share with you the three reasons (and only three reasons) you're not getting referrals – or maybe you're getting them, but the quality of them is lacking. More importantly, I will share how you can address each of these challenges.

In the end, I want you to understand precisely how referrals work. We are ALL about referrals – because they are the life blood of success in business.

My Origin Story

"Frank, why am I not getting referrals?"

I get this question often—within AmSpirit Business Connections and outside its membership. I've heard it more times than I can remember.

But I remember the first time I heard it. It was probably the most important time the question was asked.

Before I get to that, let me share a little of my backstory. I was born in Chicago, and we—my parents, older brother, and younger sister—lived a stone's throw from the Brookfield Zoo.

Chicago to Columbus

When I was five, we moved to Wisconsin, where my father pursued a Ph.D. in science education at the University of Wisconsin-Madison. Two years later, he finished his doctoral work and accepted a position as an associate professor at Michigan Technological University.

At that time, I was eight and we moved to Houghton, Michigan, an amazing little college town about four hours due north of Green Bay, Wisconsin. This is where I grew up. And Houghton is what I refer to as my hometown.

After graduating high school, I went to Beloit College, a small liberal arts college in southern Wisconsin. I studied hard, mainly because I did not want to get kicked off the football team.

But by applying myself to college, I did relatively well—actually, really well. So well, in fact, that my professors urged me to go to graduate school or law school. I did both, enrolling in a joint degree program at The Ohio State University.

3

Corporate Career to Entrepreneurial Adventure

Four years later, I had a law degree (known as a JD, or Juris Doctor) and an MBA. With those in hand, I started my career at Coopers & Lybrand (now PricewaterhouseCoopers) as a tax consultant.

It was a great job. Great pay. Great office. Great clients. Great everything – except for one thing: taxes. I didn't want to do taxes for my entire career. Most people understand that.

So, after six-and-a-half years (and a CPA designation under my belt), I left to go into private law practice. Though I started in a corporate environment, I'd always had an entrepreneurial itch I wanted to scratch. Having my own law practice seemed like a good place to start.

But a funny thing happened when I went into private practice: nothing happened. I had no idea how to get clients.

They don't teach you that in school—not in high school, college, graduate school, or law school. They don't teach it in corporate America either. For attorneys, it's especially challenging because we're not permitted to cold call, go door to door, or undertake various direct marketing initiatives.

I grew up in a science household, not a business one. We talked about chemistry, physics, and math – never business, marketing, or sales. I was under the impression that business success would simply be a matter of doing well in school, accumulating credentials, and offering a fair price. With all of that, clients would just appear.

My First Client Was, In Effect, Me

But business doesn't work that way. I was lost. I had no idea how I would survive as an attorney in private practice. At that point, I more or less asked myself, "Frank, why am I not getting referrals?"

People shared the answer with me, but I didn't hear them – or wasn't willing to listen.

- **Others**: "You should get involved with the local bar association." **ME**: Nah! Just refer me to clients."

- **Others**: "You should attend Chamber functions." **ME**: "Nah! Just refer me to clients."

- **Others**: "You should reach out and connect with strategic partners." **ME**: "Nah! Just refer me to clients."

Not surprisingly, I still wasn't getting referrals. Worse, I didn't understand why. All I really knew was that I didn't want to ask for my tax consulting job back.

But, one day I had lunch with a friend who'd take a different path out of law school. She's started her own firm and was doing well.

So, I asked her, "What do I need to do be successful?" I wanted to be referred to an impressive stable of clients like she had.

Her answer was quick. "Why don't you get into a tips club or leads group?"

Tips What? Leads Who?

I had no idea what she was talking about. But when the student is ready, the teacher appears. After all, I was quasi-desperate, so I was going to listen.

She introduced me to someone, and that person introduced me to another. Before I knew it, I was networking.

Within a week or two, I found myself at a planning meeting for a new group of a networking organization based out of Pittsburgh – Network Professionals Inc. As the local leader shared, it all made sense to me: You can lift your whole world up by helping others succeed.

For me (and likely many of you), I can talk up, promote, and even refer others all day long and feel great about it. But if I self-promote for five minutes, I'm exhausted – and all I want to do is take a nap.

So, this networking group thing was for me. I took to it like a fish to water. Helping others and trusting that goodness would come back – and it worked. I was getting referrals, good referrals. I wasn't exactly sure why, but it was happening. And that was good enough for me.

The Birth of AmSpirit Business Connections

As a result of my success, I became very involved in my group as well as the larger organization. Then in late 2003, the founder of the original organization presented me with an opportunity to purchase my operations. I wrote the biggest check I'd ever written and re-brand it as AmSpirit Business Connections.

IMPORTANT NOTE: We do nothing alone, and that's true of me too. Behind me in this networking journey has been my wife, Linda. Business insight. Financial assistance. Operation know-how. AmSpirit Business Connections is not what it is (and neither am I) without Linda. There you go, Linda – you got it in writing.

When AmSpirit Business Connections was born, I made another decision: I was going to stop the practice of law and become a student of networking. I intended to continually learn about professional relationships, business networking, and – most importantly – what drives referrals. I wanted to:

- Understand why some people had great professional relationships (and others didn't).
- Identify the practices and traits of those who have solid business networking skills.
- Master how referrals truly work.

That last point that is the genesis of this book. If you're in business and serious about success, you want referrals. In fact, that is the very basis of what AmSpirit Business Connections is about.

Over the years, I've learned a lot about why referrals happen - or don't. In this book, I'll share the insights I've gained from working with some incredibly successful entrepreneurs, sales representatives, and professionals.

Overview of the Three Reasons

"People don't give referrals because they are generally self-centered and lazy."

I've heard this statement (or something like it) from time to time. And people are sincere in saying it. After all, it's only human nature. When things don't go our way—in any situation—our first reaction is to externalize: blame others, point to situations beyond our control, or attribute it to outside forces.

But there is a simple reality when it comes to referrals, and it's this: You need to look to others to get them. So, putting the blame on others would seem to fit, right?

Wrong! Yes, you need to look to others to get referrals. After all, you can't really refer to yourself. But whether you get referral (or don't) is 100% on you. Let me repeat that, *whether you get referral (or don't) is 100% on you.*

If you aren't getting referrals, it comes down to what you do (or don't do) and what you say (or don't say).

Here's the thing. All those things you should be doing (or not doing) and what you should be saying (or getting others to say) neatly fits into one of three categories. And with that, I (again) maintain there are three reasons, and only three reasons, why you don't get referrals.

So, what are those reasons? Below is an overview of each. In the following chapters, we will explore them in more detail.

Reason #1: *Failure to Develop Relationship*

The first reason people don't get referrals is that they've failed to develop a sufficient relationship with those whom they hope will give them referrals. In short, the people they look to for referrals don't know, like, or trust them well enough.

Think about it. A consultant you've never heard of (much less met) reaches out to you via phone, e-mail or some social platform from seven states away. In short order, that consultant asks you to refer them to anybody and everybody you know.

Now, that consultant could be the absolute best at what they do. Nevertheless, you're not referring them to anyone. Why not?

You don't know them. And if you don't know them, you cannot assess whether you like them. And without the know and the like, there will be no trust. And without trust, there are no referrals.

Reason #2: *Failure to Create Recognition*

The second reason people don't get referrals is that, while they may have a trusting relationship with those they seek referrals from, they have failed to educate those same people on how to recognize a good referral for them.

Using the previous example, let's assume you know, like, and trust that consultant from seven states away. They were a college roommate, and you were inseparable for four solid years. The consultant asks you to refer them to anybody and everybody.

Under this scenario, you truly want to help the consultant—it's your good friend. You know them, like them, and trust them. Nevertheless, you still don't give them referrals. Why not?

As much as you care about your friend and roommate, you have no idea how to recognize referral opportunities for them. Consultant? That could mean a lot of things. Anybody and everybody? That doesn't help at all.

Reason #3: *Failure to Empower Engagement*

The third (and final) reason people don't get referrals is this: They may have a sufficient relationship with those from whom they hope to receive referrals. Those same people may also know how to spot great referrals for them. But they've failed to empower their referral sources with the ability to communicate about them to others.

Let's revisit the previous example—the college roommate you simply adore, the consultant from seven states away. Let's assume that this consultant has done a phenomenal job of educating you on how to recognize opportunities for them. You can spot those opportunities left and right.

The problem is that, while you can spot opportunities for the consultant, you don't know what to say. That is, you don't know how to segue into a conversation about the referral opportunity with the person (or in the situation) you're looking to refer.

The Three Reasons Summarized

These are the only three reasons, why you don't referrals:

1. Failure to Develop Relationships
2. Failure to Create Recognition
3. Failure to Empower Engagement

In the next three chapters, we will take a deeper dive into each of these reasons.

Failure to Develop Relationship

"What was the first sign of human civilization?"

This is a question that a student once asked legendary cultural anthropologist Margaret Mead. What the student wanted to know was what was the first indication that humans were different than any other animal on the planet?

As Mead gathered herself to answer, her students speculated: "Fire." "The wheel." "Tools." "Weapons." None of those, however, were Mead's answer. Her reply was, "A healed femur."

For those unfamiliar, the femur is the bone that connects the knee to the hip (commonly referred to as the thigh bone). It is the longest and strongest bone in the body of most vertebrates, including mammals, birds, reptiles, and amphibians. It plays a crucial role in supporting weight and enabling movement.

Mead explained: "When an animal breaks its femur, it's effectively a death sentence."

Think about it. Without that main bone, an animal really can't move. Thus, it can forge for food or water. And it largely loses its ability to defend itself against predators. Death is inevitable, likely within a few days.

But when anthropologists found the remains of humans with healed femurs—which, without modern medical care, requires six to eight weeks to heal—they knew there was something very different about humans. Someone (or some group) stayed behind to care for and protect their injured comrade.

Why Does This Matter?

What does this have to do with referrals? The answer lies in the profound implications of that gesture.

Let's imagine two groups of nomadic humans. Let's call one group callous and the other caring.

In the callous group, when a party member broke their femur, the remaining three would (in their way of communicating) say, "We're sorry for you, but we're moving on. It was nice knowing you."

When the callous three moved forward, they were weaker than when they were four strong. Hunting, foraging, protecting, and living became more difficult—arguably 25% more difficult. Eventually, three became two, then one, and ultimately, extinction.

Now consider the caring group. When one broke their femur, the remaining three were overcome by a powerful sense of compassion. They might not have fully understood it, but they stayed behind to protect, feed, and care for their injured comrade.

This was no small sacrifice. A successful existence at the time required a nomadic lifestyle, so staying put for 60 days was a significant risk. Despite this, the caring group stayed.

When their injured member healed, they moved forward "four strong"—33% stronger than the callous group. Additionally, the three who stayed behind gained a loyal comrade who would help them in their time of need.

These factors—strength and compassion—increased the likelihood of survival for the caring group. Their genes carried on, while the callous group's DNA went extinct.

In short, compassion became a survival trait. Whether consciously or subconsciously, people chose to associate with those who would care for them in times of need—and they reciprocated. A simple word for these mutual commitments is relationships.

The Link Between Relationships and Referrals

Fast forward to today: Regardless of gender, religion, race, or whatever, that pro-caring DNA is coursing through your veins – and everyone else's. Whether or not you realize it or not, you seek to align yourself with people who are willing to (metaphorically) stay behind when you break your femur. And those people are looking for the same.

To get referrals, the first thing you need to do is build relationships.

Remember the example of the consultant? The one you've never met who reaches out via phone, email, or social media from seven states away? Even if that consultant is the absolute best at what they do, you're not referring them to anyone because you don't know, like, or trust them.

To get referrals, you need people to "know, like, and trust" you. But how can you accomplish that?

Foundational Networking

This question is one I addressed in my book, *Foundational Networking: Building Know, Like and Trust to Create a Lifetime of Extraordinary Success*. While I encourage you to read it (and I'll elaborate below), the core idea can be summed up in one phrase:

Become the person you want to associate with!

Stop looking for that knight in shining armor who will serve to lift you out of your professional woes. Rather than looking, become that person.

People naturally gravitate toward individuals who embody the qualities they admire. Everyone wants to know that person. They can't help but like that person. And they quickly trust that person.

Who Do You Want to Network With?

Think about the kind of person you'd want to associate with. It has nothing to do with personal characteristics, like height or appearance. Hollywood might value "tall, dark, and handsome," but that doesn't necessarily make someone knowable, likable, or trustworthy.

And the same is true for education. Smart people can be unlikable, and honorable people might not be traditionally "wise."

Chances are, you want to associate with people who exhibit certain **attitudes** and **habits** that foster knowing, liking, and trusting.

In *Foundational Networking*, I broke these relationship-building attitudes and habits down into three basic categories or components: **presence**, **altruism**, and **integrity**. Let's explore each.

Presence

> Presence involves your attitudes and habits—how you carry yourself and how you appear to others.
>
> As humans, the most important question we subconsciously ask about others is, metaphorically speaking: "Will this person stay with me if I break my femur?" From the moment you come onto someone's

radar, they begin determining whether they can know, like, and trust you.

This assessment often happens subconsciously, even before you've said anything and sometimes even before you've walked into the room or joined a Zoom meeting. People observe your social media, listen to how others talk about you, and notice how you carry yourself—how you write emails, answer the phone, or start a conversation, whether in person or online.

They're trying to answer many questions: Are you stoic or friendly? Are you exasperated or interested? Are you hurried or calm? These first impressions are critical, but they're just the beginning.

Beyond those initial impressions, people continue forming opinions about you through future interactions—whether in person, over the phone, or online. Their conclusions center on various clues, including your facial expressions, posture, and tone of voice. In essence, they're deciding whether you're someone they want to associate with.

There's nothing wrong with this; in fact, you do the same thing. You're constantly making assessments and evaluations of others.

Becoming the Person Others Want to Associate With

Take a moment to visualize someone you want to associate with or someone you already have a relationship with. Chances are, they exude confidence or carry a certain uplifting energy. You're not imagining someone who is perpetually down or moody, right?

Instead, you likely envision someone whose presence uplifts you—someone who makes you feel more optimistic, determined, and confident when you're around them.

If you want that in your network, it's reasonable to conclude that others want the same. They, too, want to surround themselves with individuals who have this presence.

You attract the kind of person you are. So, if you want to connect with uplifting, inspiring people, you need to become that kind of person.

Presence Is About Projection, Not Words

Your presence has very little to do with what you say and almost everything to do with how you project certain qualities. Researchers estimate that more than 90% of what we communicate is nonverbal.

The good news? You can improve or enhance your presence by adopting certain attitudes and habits. These habits project to others that you're someone they want to associate with.

Most of these attitudes and habits are neither complicated nor difficult to adopt. In fact, you may already exhibit many of them from time to time.

Again, presence is the impression you leave on others, whether through in-person contact or communication (in any form). Below are some key attitudes and habits, drawn from my book *Foundational Networking*, that you can develop and maintain to draw others to you.

Key Attitudes and Habits to Cultivate

- **Have a High Personal Expectation**: Always strive to achieve more in life, both personally and professionally. Be the person who's working toward and expecting to achieve something extraordinary – writing a book, training for a marathon, launching a new initiative, or something else. Successful people want to associate with others who are striving for greatness. Become that person.

- **Be Accepting of Your Situation**: While striving to achieve more, accept where you are in your journey. Life won't always go your way—so what? Take setbacks in stride, turn the page, and focus on what's next. People are attracted to eternal optimism and are more comfortable associating with it.

- **Become Contagiously Energetic**: Life is hard— for you and everyone else. That's why people gravitate toward those who seem ready to take on any challenge. Energized individuals, who lean into their tasks with enthusiasm, inspire and motivate others simply through their presence. Become one of those people.

- **Have a Sense of Humor**: Everyone loves to laugh, and people are drawn to those who make them feel comfortable enough to laugh. Use humor thoughtfully, but don't shy away from it—it's a powerful tool for building connections.

- **Be Authentic**: Always present a true reflection of who you are. Don't try to morph into someone else based on the situation or the people around you. Consistency in how you present yourself helps others trust you. Not everyone will vibe with you, and that's okay— there are plenty of people who will.

- **Be Happy**: While people may care about others during tough times, no one wants to associate with someone who is perpetually downtrodden. People want to surround themselves with happy individuals. Focus on what makes you happy, appreciate your life, and keep a smile on your face. Your happiness will not only improve your day but also draw others to you.

- **Be Humble**: Take pride in who you are and what you do but recognize that you're no better than anyone else. Everyone has unique value to add to the world. People appreciate humility and are naturally drawn to those who stay grounded.

Final Thoughts

This isn't an exhaustive list, but it gives you the gist. In summary, ask yourself what you admire about how others show up in the world. Then work to adopt those same qualities to enhance your own presence.

Altruism

In the earliest years of human existence, people discovered they could improve their chances of survival—and increase their level of prosperity—by sharing labor, tools, and information.

However, chances of survival only increased if one was interacting with someone who was willing to contribute to the "greater good" of the community. If someone contributed to another who was unwilling to reciprocate in some form, that contribution became a detriment.

From this reality, humans developed a keen ability to identify those who were altruistic—willing to sacrifice for the benefit of their small societies. These altruistic individuals became the people they kept in their world. And for those who didn't have a community to belong to, survival was short-lived.

While today it's not a matter of survival, success and prosperity still depend on similar principles. People naturally want to interact with and contribute to those who are also willing to give. This is human nature. Altruism is essential to building relationships, and relationships are the foundation of success.

The Golden Rule of Networking

Once you understand this idea, you need to strive to embody it. Become the kind of person whose attitudes and habits focus on contributing to others. This principle is referred to as the "Golden Rule of Networking," which is summarized as "give first; get second."

In her book *People Power, Donna Fisher* refers to this as the "Boomerang Effect:" When you take the initiative to give, participate, and offer support to your network, it's like throwing a boomerang. Eventually, what you inject into your network—opportunities, information, support, energy, and connections—returns to you.

Developing Altruistic Attitudes and Habits

To attract people to you, it's important to cultivate attitudes and habits that make you more giving (altruistic). While you should never give with the expectation of receiving, people are often eager to reciprocate. Why?

1. **Your altruistic attitude rubs off on them.** Over time, people tend to mimic the behaviors of those they admire.

2. **They want to remain in your world**. Contributing to your life ensures that relationship continues.

In *Foundational Networking*, I explore altruism in detail. For now, here's a summary:

- Altruism goes beyond the transfer of wealth.

- Altruism exists on a spectrum; everyone is altruistic to some degree, but some are more so than others.

- Altruism means serving others beyond what you do professionally.

When you embrace the idea that giving to others is the key to building great personal and professional relationships, two key questions arise:

1) How can I develop a more giving mindset?
2) What are things that I give to others?

Developing a Giving Mindset

A few years after writing *Foundational Networking*, I began questioning whether I truly had a giving mindset. As humans, we often delude ourselves about our own behaviors.

To challenge myself, I began tracking and recording what I did for others. By keeping a journal of my altruistic actions, I became more service oriented.

This journey of self-discovery is documented in my book *The Giving Journal*. The beauty of this book? I give it away for free. You can download it at *The Giving Journal* (https://www.amspirit.com/blog/the-giving-journal). Enjoy—and share the gift by telling others about it.

Ways to Give Without Financial Cost

As to the second question - What can you give to others? – here's a rundown of ways to be altruistic. None require financial resources; they simply require time and intentionality:

- **Compassion**: Look around. There are people with challenges – stresses, insecurities, struggles, regrets, and disappointments. Ask yourself how you can alleviate their pain.

- **Encouragement**: Providing moral support in tough times, even if that's all you can do, can be invaluable.

- **Smiles**: A simple smile can brighten someone's day. When you smile, others often smile back, gaining an uplifting feeling.

- **Volunteer**: Donate your time and talents to charitable organizations, civic associations, or schools. This strengthens your network while helping others.

- **Compliments**: Offering genuine compliments costs nothing but can improve someone's self-esteem.

- **Accolades**: Celebrate others' achievements. This reinforces your relationship and builds trust.

- **Appreciation**: Express gratitude through spoken words, written notes, or small gestures. Saying "thank you" shows others you value them.

- **Attention**: Listen actively. Seek to understand, clarify, and show genuine interest in what others share. This validates their feelings.

- **Receiving**: Oddly enough, allowing others to help you can be a gift in itself. It gives them the joy of contributing to your life.

- **Thoughtfulness**: Look for ways to be considerate of others' feelings and find small ways to positively impact their lives.

- **Introductions**: Bringing people together from different parts of your life offers tremendous value. Connections are gifts that keep giving.

Giving Without Being Asked

There are countless ways to be altruistic, and most cost nothing but time. As you practice giving, strive to do so without waiting to be asked. These unprompted acts of generosity often leave the most lasting impressions.

Integrity

Integrity involves your attitudes and habits regarding how you interact with others.

In one sense, integrity is straightforward—you know it when you see it. Yet, in another sense, it can be complex. How do you describe it? That answer isn't always clear.

In *Foundational Networking*, I argue that integrity is more important than your altruism or presence. You can maintain some semblance of a network without an ounce of altruism. Similarly, a lack of positive presence, while detrimental, isn't catastrophic.

However, without integrity, you have nothing. People will simply not look past this deficiency. It's like the number zero: any number multiplied by zero equals zero. Without integrity, all your other positive attributes are meaningless.

Integrity Is Tested in Small Moments

It's important to note that people don't measure your integrity based on major interactions or significant transactions. Instead, they gauge it through smaller, everyday tests. Consider these examples:

- Are you the type to stand patiently in a long line, or do you try to connive your way closer to the front?

- Do you pay a late fee without complaint, or do you seek a waiver through excuses or threats?

- When a cashier undercharges you, do you point out the mistake, or do you accept the benefit of the error?

People focus on the small things because most people don't fail the big tests. For example, if someone entrusts you with a large sum of money for escrow or as a down payment, you likely handle it appropriately. While there are rare cases of business types absconding with funds, these situations represent an incredibly small fraction of cases.

For the most part, people demonstrate appropriate personal and professional integrity in major transactions. As such, these situations aren't what others use to judge your integrity.

Instead, they observe the small things—and those small things can have significant consequences.

The Impact of Small Acts

The short poetic fable *For Want of a Nail* illustrates the ripple effect of seemingly minor actions:

> For want of a nail, the shoe was lost;
> For want of a shoe, the horse was lost;
> For want of the horse, the rider was lost;
> For want of the rider, the battle was lost;
> For want of the battle, the kingdom was lost;
> And all for the want of a nail.

The moral of this poetic fable is that the little things you do (or fail to do) serve to bolster or undermine how others perceive your integrity. And that perception has broader implications as to how people see you, trust you, and ultimately refer you – or don't.

Habits and Attitudes to Build Integrity

Here are key habits and attitudes that can help you demonstrate integrity and strengthen your relationships:

- **Offer Trust**: If you want others to trust you, you must trust them first. People are more likely to trust and associate with those who extend trust to them.

- **Share Credit**: Acknowledge the contributions of others in your successes. Sharing credit energizes people and strengthens their appreciation of you.

- **Reliability**: The greatest compliment is being known as reliable. When you consistently follow through on your commitments, others feel confident turning to you—or referring others to you.

- **Honesty**: Choose sincerity and truthfulness, even when no one else would know otherwise. By consistently choosing honesty, you build long-term credibility.

- **Contrition**: When you make a mistake, don't hesitate to say, "I'm sorry." Apologizing disarms anger and reinforces your character.

- **Be Accountable**: Instead of blaming others for misfortunes, first examine your own contribution to the situation. This self-awareness promotes growth and preserves relationships.

- **Freely Forgive**: Forgiving others helps you redirect energy toward more productive endeavors and fosters a sense of comfort for those associating with you.

- **Be Open-Minded**: Respectfully share your opinions while recognizing they're not definitive facts. When you encounter differing views, agree to disagree and seek common ground. This builds rapport and mutual respect.

- **Use Tact**: Think carefully before acting or speaking. Tact requires consideration, kindness, and reason, ensuring your actions are perceived positively.

- **Motivate Appropriately**: Avoid manipulation and focus on objectives that benefit everyone. True motivation aligns the goals of all involved parties.

- **Influence Responsibly**: Use your influence ethically, without coercion. By doing so, you'll gain admiration, respect, and trust.

- **Provide Consistent Comfort**: The way you make others feel during interactions shapes their perception of your integrity. Strive to make others feel comfortable and valued.

The Three Keys to Building Relationships

Building relationships with others—getting them to know, like, and trust you—is the first step to receiving referrals. This process depends on cultivating attitudes and habits in three key areas:

1) **Presence**: How you show up in the world and the impression you leave on others.
2) **Altruism**: How you contribute your time, energy, and resources to others.
3) **Integrity**: How others perceive you interact with them and others.

By focusing on these attributes, you'll create strong, meaningful relationships—both personally and professionally.

However, relationships alone aren't enough to secure referrals. You might think they would be, but there's more to it. Read on …

Failure to Create Recognition

"You know, I like to think my parents loved me. I really do."

This is something I often say when I talk about getting referrals. It's a near-perfect lead-in to help people understand that having a great relationship isn't enough. So, let me explain.

Sincerely, I like to think my parents loved me. They said so, and there were many signs they did. For starters, they brought me into the world and raised me.

That was no small thing. They made sure I had decent clothes and was well-fed. With their encouragement (and tough love), I graduated high school. They were instrumental in getting me through college and law school. Over the years, they helped me in dozens of other ways.

Thinking about it, my parents did love me. They did. I'm confident of that. In truth, I had a great relationship with them.

But you know what? As great as our relationship was, my parents never referred me. Not once. Not ever.

Now, I never expected referrals from them. But I use this to illustrate a point: It's entirely possible to have a great relationship with someone—people who genuinely care about you—and still not receive referrals.

While I didn't expect referrals from my parents, there's a reason they didn't happened. Our interactions revolved around watching sports, cooking, and home improvement projects. We never talked business. I never took the time to educate them on how to recognize opportunities for me.

Relationship Is Not Enough

So, if you have great relationships with people who aren't giving you referrals, it might be because you haven't helped them see how they can.

I experienced this firsthand. When I joined a Chapter of what's now AmSpirit Business Connections as a new business attorney, I thought I was doing everything right. I built relationships, was asked to be Chapter President, gave referrals, brought guests, and made sure to arrive early and stay late to connect with others. People knew me, liked me, and trusted me. Yet, I didn't receive many referrals—and the few I got weren't useful.

The problem? I did a terrible job of asking for referrals. People had no idea how they could help me.

At this point, you might say, "Whoa, Frank! That's not me. I've got a great 30-second commercial. I even took a course and had professional help. People love it. I won a contest!"

Great. But let's talk about those 30-second commercials. It's not just about having one; it's about crafting it thoughtfully.

You Need a Great 30-Second Commercial

Having a solid 30-second commercial is essential, especially early in a relationship, when someone asks, "What do you do?"

In that moment, you can't afford to fumble or ramble. You need to be ready with a concise, polished response that clearly explains who you are and what you do.

For example, you might say ... "I assist clients with buying and selling homes, guiding them through every step of the real estate process."

But here's the thing: Business seldom transpires on that initial encounter. Neither do referrals happen.

Rather it takes a second interaction - or a third, or maybe even a 14th – before solid business, great referrals, or productive introductions happen. After all, to receive these things, you need to have a relationship. That is, people need to know, like and trust you.

The Problem with That 30-Second Commercial

So, what are you supposed to do in all those subsequent encounters? You know, during the second meeting? Or the third, fourth, fifth, etc. It's during these interactions that the people you're hoping will help you would like to learn a little more about how they can. What are you supposed to say?

Well, the answer is *not* launching into that 30-second commercial – no matter how polished it is – over and over again.

> You know, **"I assist clients with buying and selling ..."** blah, blah, blah.

Surely, you get the point. That would be annoying and not productive at all.

That was my problem. Over time, I had crafted a well-polished rendition of who I was and what it did (and practiced it often).

> "I'm Frank Agin, an attorney who provides legal services for the life of your business. A good referral for me is any business that needs legal help."

As 30-second commercials go, mine was arguable not horrible. But it didn't say a whole lot. And saying it over and over, week after week (in our Chapter meeting) didn't change things. Afterall, if you're doing something wrong, doing it more doesn't fix the situation.

Moving Beyond That 30-Second Commercial

And that's the case with lots of people. Like me, they create a strong 30-second commercial and think that they're all set. They proudly recite it over and over. And when nothing comes from it, they endure increasing levels of frustration (and ultimately declare that networking doesn't work).

Instead, when you're interacting with someone you already know—perhaps at a periodic meeting of a referral-based networking organization—it's time to graduate from that trusty 30-second commercial. In its place, you need to embark on different messaging strategies that will greatly increase the likelihood of referrals.

My advice, if you're moving beyond the initial conversation stage with someone, is to ditch the notion of relying on that one great 30-second commercial. Instead, be ready with dozens of mediocre messages that effectively communicate the types of referrals you're looking to get.

> **"Yeah, yeah, Frank. You're so full of it. Everybody gets me. My messaging is just fine. The reason people don't give me referrals is that they are generally only out for themselves."**

Yes, someone said this to me. And I couldn't disagree more.

People Want to Help You

Remember the notion of the healed femur. We are looking for people who are willing to help us in our time of need (and that need comes in lots of shapes and sizes).

On some level most humans realize that they need to contribute to the lives of others first. So, people are not generally only out for themselves. In fact, I'm willing to bet that those with whom you have a relationship—the ones who know, like, and trust you—really want to help you.

And the reason they don't is the same reason my parents never gave me a referral: Because you've failed to sufficiently educate your network on how to recognize opportunities for you.

If you're with me and accept the notion to message better to get referrals, you might be wondering, "Well, how? I feel as if I'm doing the best I can."

You probably are. But there is always room for improvement. After all, I'm writing this, and I still struggle with practical applications of creating recognition.

This is a "work on it continually" sort of thing—not a "set it and forget it" one. To address the notion of creating recognition, there's a lot to unpack. Let's get started.

What follows are a series of sections. Each one contains a lesson or two that can help you get your network (those people who know, like, and trust you) to have a better understanding as to who they can refer to you.

Be Specific, And Nothing but Specific

If you truly want referrals, then the first thing you need to do is stop asking to be introduced to the Three Stooges. And no, I'm not talking about Curly, Moe, and Larry. – I mean asking for *anyone*, *someone*, and *everyone* (or their close cousins: *anybody*, *somebody*, and *everybody*).

These are indefinite pronouns. In English, they refer to nonspecific people or things. Because they don't point to a particular individual or object (and instead imply generality or uncertainty), the human brain struggles to process them.

This is precisely why repeatedly stating "A good referral for me is anyone who needs an attorney," led to only frustration.

Think about it like this. When you go into a restaurant and the server asks, "Can I take your order?" If you respond with, "Please bring me something to eat," you are likely to get nothing. Instead, you need to be specific. "I'd like the chicken fajitas with corn tortillas, and no sour cream, please." Asking for referrals works the same way.

Years ago, Gina Winterstein, owner of Panagea Networks (a telecommunication consulting company and franchisee within AmSpirit Business Connections) shared a great example. She said, "If you tell me that you're looking for a used car, I will drive around seeing lots of them and never think about you. But if you tell me that you're looking for a pink VW bug, the moment I see one, you'll immediately come to mind."

Being specific arms your network's reticular activation system (RAS). The RAS is a brain network that filters information and prioritizes what's important. When the prompt is "used cars," the term is too vague to arm Gina's RAS. So, as she drives, she sees countless cars, but her brain doesn't filter any of that information for you.

When the prompt is "pink VW bug," Gina's RAS is armed and ready. And when she sees ones, metaphorically bells go off in her head. That's the power of being specific.

When I say, "be specific," I don't mean describing your business operations in minute detail (e.g., "We're ready to do legal work seven days a week, with a state-of-the-art computer system"). Instead, be clear about the kinds of situations in which you serve clients. More on that later.

We consistently preached the notion of being specific within AmSpirit Business Connections. When someone isn't, we'll politely pull them aside after a meeting (or reach out privately). After all, letting someone continue being counterproductive isn't doing them any favors.

One day, I listen to Rachel Luther share about her virtual assistant business, Check Off Your List. While she was (and is) passionate about serving clients, her messaging was vague and full of indefinite pronouns. Doing what we do, I reached out afterward to offer help.

She thought about what I had to say and politely responded, "Oh, Frank, you don't understand. What I do is so diverse that I *have* to be vague."

I replied, "Maybe, but my brain doesn't do vague. Nobody's brain does. And just because you feel you need to be vague, doesn't change neuroscience and how people comprehend information."

The truth is, when it comes to messaging to others about how to spot referral for you, the onus is on you to adjust your message to their level of understanding. It's not their responsibility to raise their level of understanding to suit you.

But as accurate as that might be, the truth alone wasn't going to help Rachel get more referrals. So, I simply asked her this: "Can you tell me about a client you're working with?"

She relaxed a bit, saying, "Sure. We work with lots of small non-profits. You see, most have volunteer boards and only parttime paid support. Those organizations use us to handle various details between board meetings."

That statement sent off alarms in my RAS. You see, since 2015, I've helped facilitate The Charitable Roundtable – a monthly gathering of non-profits from around the U.S. While I didn't know of a specific organization needing help, I let her know about the opportunity.

Later that week, I was talking to a business banker. I shared about my conversation with Rachel. The moment I mentioned her work with small nonprofits, the banker interrupted: "Please introduce me to Rachel! I have a lot of small nonprofit clients, and they're a mess. They need someone like her."

That's the power of being specific.

Avoid Techno, Whiz-bang Jargon

I often tell people that they have a choice. They can sound smart, or they can get referrals. Generally, both won't happen.

I see more people lose referrals by using jargon than for any other reason. Often, they don't realize they're doing it, but the result is the same—no referrals.

One morning, I was attending a Chapter of AmSpirit Business Connections. During the referral segment, a young financial advisor stood up and said, "A good referral for me is anyone struggling with RMDs," then sat down.

I don't usually call people out publicly, but I had just trained the group on avoiding jargon, and this Chapter had a good-natured vibe. So, I said, "Kevin, please stand back up." He smiled, unsure of what was coming.

I asked the Chapter, "Who knows what an RMD is?" Everyone laughed and shook their heads. No one had a clue. Kevin laughed, too, realizing his mistake.

"Kevin, please tell everyone what an RMD is," I said.

"Okay, it's a required minimum distribution," Kevin shared in a matter-of-fact tone, as if that would totally clarify things. Then he sat back down.

"Kevin, please stand back up." Everybody laughed, as did Kevin. I asked the Chapter, "Who here knows what a required minimum distribution is?" Nobody did.

"Kevin, in layman's terms, please explain."

Kevin elaborated:

> "When you save for retirement with accounts like a 401(k) or traditional IRA, you defer taxes, letting your savings grow tax-free. But the government doesn't let you avoid taxes forever. At age 73, you

must start withdrawing money each year—these withdrawals are called required minimum distributions, or RMDs. Without proper planning, this can create significant tax problems."

And just like that, Kevin created several "a-ha" moments in the room. Instead of leaving people quietly confused, he helped them think of people who might need his help.

If you think, "Well, people should speak up if they don't understand," here's the reality: People are nice. They won't risk embarrassing you by admitting their confusion.

Even if you ask them directly – "do you understand what I mean? – they'll likely say they do, even if they don't. They don't want to embarrass themselves as being ignorant on something.

As a result, you let your network know what you're looking for and they have zero clue as to what you seek. As such, the net effect is that you don't get referrals.

Don't feel bad. Most people come by talking in jargon honestly. Think about it. You know your craft well, right? You likely have years of experience. And preceding that, you endured intense education (and maybe had to pass a test or some other rite of passage).

And you're uber passion about what you do. You devote 50-60 hours a week to doing what you do. And when you're not working, you likely thinking about your craft, mulling over how you can innovate and serve better.

And much of that time you're working, you're around others who do what you do. And while you speak English, it's a special dialect of English that is somewhat skewed towards accounting, law, mortgage, insurance, or whatever. And that dialect is laced with terms and acronyms that help you communicate in shorthand.

For example, at the office Kevin tells his assistant, "Set up a call with the Johnson's to review their RMD situation." He understands. His assistant understands. So, it would be pointless to ask his assistant to set up a call with a client call and then launching into a 50-word description of required minimum distribution.

So, because you're so entrenched in what you do, and know it so well, you just forget that most people don't know it like you do. Think about it. A plumber thinks and talks about plumbing continually throughout the week. You only think about it when the toilet won't flush.

That was me when I was practicing attorney in a Chapter all those years ago. Because I talked legalese for three years of law school and three months while I studied for the bar exam and six years working in a big firm environment, I assumed how I talked was commonplace. It wasn't. Not even close.

Worse yet, no one told me. They were being nice. Or they were afraid that maybe they were the only ones who didn't understand, and they didn't want to embarrass themselves by asking.

Whatever the case, I wasn't get many referrals. And the ones I did receive were not great. And that's true of anyone who insists on using techno, whiz-bang jargon.

Again, you can sound smart, or you can get referrals. Generally, both won't happen.

Don't Give Them Everything (Including the Kitchen Sink)

You'd think that once you're messaging to ask for referrals is specific and void of techno, whiz-bang jargon you'd be all set. After all, at this point, you'd be able to craft a series of great messages to share out to your network contacts.

That was my thinking, anyway. Until I went into a Chapter of AmSpirit Business Connections to conduct an exercise. In the exercise, I handed out a flyer that instructed members to develop a list of specific referral message ideas. I didn't intend for them to create full-blown 30-second commercials, just a list of directions they could pursue.

After about five minutes, I asked if anyone would like to share something they'd come up with. I was hoping for one revelation from their few minutes of brainstorming. Quickly, someone volunteered – the woman who held the mortgage lender category in the Chapter.

"Ok, give us something," I encouraged.

She started in, "This is a great exercise. I've come up with 15." Then she proceeded to rip through her complete list, like an auctioneer. Everything she shared was relatively specific and each without any sort of jargon.

But here's the problem (and it's a brain problem). When you fire out a list of referral requests to your network (no matter how specific and jargon-free) you trip up people's thinking machines.

Think about it. When you share out that first decent message (e.g., "the person who's lived in their home for more than three years and has built-up equity"), the human brain takes that information and runs it through your networking partner's RAS.

You remember the RAS. It serves as sort of a mental Rolodex or CRM. As such, your networking partner's brain compares the information requested (e.g., "homeowner greater than three years") against the litany of people in their brain. It then identifies potential referral targets. Pretty simple.

Here's the problem, when you mention the second item on the list, that mental Rolodex starts over (even if it hasn't completed the first query). Then the third item derails the process again. Quickly, your networking partner's brain realizes it cannot keep up and so it sort of shuts down. It might be listening, but it's not processing.

So, I encourage you to share out referral asks one at a time (and not in a list). This certainly works well with a format like AmSpirit Business Connections, where the referral group meets weekly.

But this same logic applies even if you don't belong to a networking organization (or you're looking to be effective at asking for referrals outside your Chapter of AmSpirit Business Connections). Now, you might think, "But I only get an opportunity with this super connected person occasionally. I need to lay it all out there."

Do you really? Remember, your needs do not circumvent brain science. I would encourage you to consider who you're talking to (and the situation) and limit what you have to say to what fits best.

For example, if you're a financial advisor and having a conversation with a young professional who is likely connected to other young professionals, you don't want to yammer on about how wonderful you are with required minimum distributions. Rather, you might say something like (and note that it's sandwiched between a reference to that you do a whole lot more):

> "Our firm does lots of different things. But lately, we've been helping a lot of clients with young children get focused on investing to meet the cost of college. But again, that's just one of many things we do."

Depending on the length of the meeting or encounter, you might share out one or two other things. But it's pointless to spew out a litany of referral requests (effectively, giving them a verbal brochure). The only thing that the person will remember is that you sound desperate.

Be Your Own Tough Russian Judge

We humans are generally terrible at judging ourselves. In fact, we're downright delusional by nature.

But if you want referrals — and if you've read this far, I assume you do — you need to put in the hard work of educating people on how to recognize opportunities for you.

This requires continually improving your messaging. You need to closely examine what you say and how others might hear it.

As an example, I was once talking with someone in AmSpirit Business Connections and sharing about how messaging is so important to getting referrals. Be specific. No jargon. One topic at a time.

This particular member totally agreed. He then went on to tell me, "I am specific. You see, I focus exclusively on small businesses that are profit-oriented, with at least 25 employees." And he was totally convinced that his messaging was great.

In my opinion, it wasn't. So, I politely pushed back. It would have been a disservice to him – and his Chapter – if I hadn't.

After thinking a bit, I shared, "What you're asking for is akin is asking for a car, with four, round wheels and a 1.5-liter engine."

He gave me a confused look, so I went on to explain. "If someone asks for a car, the request is very broad, and somewhat vague. There are lots of cars. They come in various shapes and sizes. The ask is so broad that people's brains cannot frame a search.

"Qualifying the request with 'four round wheels' doesn't help. That's the basic definition of a car.

"And asking for a car with a 1.5-liter engine? That's specific, but the average person doesn't know a car's engine size. Sure, they could research it—but no one has that kind of time just to accommodate someone's random ask."

He was still puzzled, so I related it to his messaging.

I explained that, according to the U.S. Small Business Administration, 95% of businesses in the United States are small businesses. So, when he said he worked with "small businesses," he was being too broad and vague.

As for "profit-oriented businesses," I asked, "Who isn't profit-oriented? Even nonprofits aim to have their revenues exceed expenses. 'Profit-oriented' is as helpful as 'four round wheels' to describe a car."

And while "businesses with at least 25 employees" seemed like a good qualifier, I pointed out that few people know how many employees a company has. Sure, they could research it, but they're unlikely to do so for a referral.

This conversation inspired the member to develop themes for his messaging. He assigned themes to months throughout the year and crafted three or four messages for each.

In summary, he committed to putting in the work to refine his messaging—and he understood the importance of being self-critical. You can't assume your messaging is perfect or good enough.

The practice of refining your messaging isn't about how or what you communicate—it's about how your audience receives it.

That's what makes this difficult. You know exactly what you mean, but you can't assume others interpret it the same way.

There's no easy answer. It takes continual thought ("How can I be clearer about what I'm looking for?") and action to improve.

Stop Telling Me What You Do!

When asking for referrals, many people fall into the trap of answering a variation of the "What do you do?" question.

For example, a real estate agent might say:

> "I'm a real estate agent. I help people and families find the home of their dreams."

Or

> "I assist clients with buying and selling homes, guiding them through every step of the real estate process."

Or

> "I match people with their ideal homes, ensuring they find a property that suits their lifestyle and budget."

Or

> "I work as a real estate consultant, providing clients with insights on buying, selling, and investing in real estate."

Each of these is a decent description of *what* the real estate agent does. But they all say the same thing – the real estate agent serves as an intermediary between people buying and selling properties.

And people hear the same thing over and over, they get bored. And when they get bored, they stop listening.

Worst of all, these *what* statement don't help your network recognize referrals opportunities for you, as they do very little to enlighten people on the value you offer.

Instead of telling people *what* you do, make your messaging about "when" you do it.

What? When? Huh? Let's quickly explore. A *what* statement is a general explanation of your role, or it could be a job description, or it might be the business objectives, or even a mission statement.

When statements don't relate to a point on the calendar or time on a clock. Instead, *when* statements focus on context rather than just the role or service itself.

- They can describe specific situations or problems where a particular service or solution is needed.

- They can also specify a target audience and a common challenge or pain point it faces.

- They can also offer a relatable scenario and illustrate how a particular service would be beneficial.

The important difference is that if you use *what* statements, the things you share tend to slip out of people's minds. If, however, you use *when* statements, the things you share tends to embed themselves in people's minds.

Think of this in terms of Teflon versus Velcro. Teflon is a non-stick, heat-resistant coating used on cookware. On the other hand, Velcro is a reusable fastening system.

As an example of *what* (Teflon) versus *when* (Velcro), consider how a real estate agent might message:

- **Teflon** (What): I help people looking to buy or sell a home.

- **Velcro** (When): I help families that are moving mom into a home, as they are likely going to need to do something with her house.

Most importantly, using *when* statements, you effectively place little reminders in your network's brain. And these memories then sit quietly in their heads just waiting for that instant when they seize upon something you've told them to look or listen for.

An even more powerful thing about statements of when is that you literally have dozens and dozens of different circumstances, situations, and scenarios to share.

For example, our hypothetical real estate agent could ask for a referral by saying …

> "Refer me to those new parents that live in a tiny apartment with a screaming baby. I can help find that starter home that will return a little sanity to their world."

> Or

> "Refer me to those families looking to get into the Jefferson Township School District. I can help them network into that community, as I grew up there and have loads of contacts."

Or

"Refer me to that family who've shared that they would like to have a weekend getaway place. I can help as I'm part of a network of realtors specializing in these sorts of properties."

Or

"Refer me to that end-nester couple that indicates that they are tired of cleaning a big house and maintaining the yard that comes with it. wants, I can help. In the last year I helped a dozen plus older couples downsize to a place that has minimal housework."

And the real estate agent could go on and on with this list. But so could you. Think about it. Just as every person that a real estate agent helps to buy or sell a home does so for a different reason, every customer or client you serve has a different story has to how and why you serve them.

And each of these different stories can be crafted into a statement of when that you can share with your network.

- Tell your network about the situations *when* you serve others.
- Tell your network about the scenarios *when* you add massive value.
- Tell your network about the circumstances *when* you change lives.

And because each is message is different, they become compelling. Thus, your network is listening and remembering. This, in time, leads to more and better referrals.

NOTE: If you have time to take an eight-minute break, watch this video … *Talking in When's*:

https://www.youtube.com/watch?v=8DSMvwnC2zs

Capitalize on the Power of 30-Second Stories

For some reason, people tend to ask for referrals using abstract narratives, which sound like:

"We're looking to be connected to home builders, as through our software system we can help them operate more effectively."

But the reality is that they'd be more effective asking if they wrapped that story in a narrative. Something like:

"Last quarter, through our software system, we helped ABC Home Construction identify potential downtime amongst its field teams. This helped them save over $10,000 a month in unproductive labor costs."

So, part of the work you need to do to better educate your network on how to recognize referrals for you, is to craft 30-second stories.

Storytelling is more effective than abstract communication for lots of reasons. Mainly because it engages the listener emotionally. Thus, it aligns with the cognitive processes that uses vivid imagery.

Research shows that narratives lead to better comprehension and recall. When you use a 30-second story, your audience is more likely to understand and remember what you've said—ultimately resulting in more referrals.

The great thing about stories is that you already have plenty of material to work with.

Think about it. Every client (or customer if you prefer that term) can be a story. For example, as an attorney I helped lots of clients purchase businesses. But each of those clients had a different nuance to their situation. And thus, I had material for various stories, each talking about something different to look for.

In addition, a different service (or interaction) with a particular client can be a separate story. For example, if one of those people I helped purchase a business wanted me to do some estate planning, that could be another story.

Or perhaps you present a client with various options, and they go with one. You can still craft the options they declined into stories. For example, in doing estate planning for that client, I share that they can go with a simple will or a trust. Whatever the client selects, I have two stories I can craft.

Beyond your own clients, colleagues can be a source of stories. When I practiced law, other attorneys often shared their experiences with me. I could turn those into examples or articles. Seminars, trade publications, or even hypothetical scenarios you think up during idle moments can also provide material.

You can create stories from situations and scenarios that you concoct in mind during those idle moments on your commute or while walking. This is not lying, and no one is going to audit you ("Who was the person you transferred a liquor license for, Frank? We need to know. We don't believe you.").

Rather, you're showing the people you're seeking referrals from how they can recognize them. You're crafting stories about things you know you can do but may not have done yet.

For example, before I ever set up a trust for a client, I'd taken a class on it, study about it for the bar exam, and talked with other attorneys. I knew exactly what I needed to do and could serve any referral well (and did). And the same is likely true for you.

- A real estate agent can ask for a referral to sell a condo not ever having sold a condo.

- An accountant can ask for a referral to do a non-profit tax return not ever having done one.

- A financial advisor can ask for a referral to help a family invest for college not ever done so.

And, with these stories, you don't need to couch or qualify your words (i.e., Well, um, I've never done a trust before, but ...). Own your story. Be confident. Most everyone you look to get referral from don't have the knowledge or experience you do. For example:

> "Last week, I helped a client purchase the business his parents built. We set everything up, so the business name was the same, my client now is the owner, and the parents are set for life with a stream of income. If you know of a person who

50

might be hoping to take over a business from mom and dad, I would appreciate an introduction."

In summary, you have access to a wealth of stories to help you message for potential referrals. You simply need to decide that you're going to craft and deploy them. And since stories can be highly effective in helping you get referrals, why wouldn't you?

Deploy Figurative Language

Think about how you learned. You were taught the ABCs. From that, you learned that each of those letters had an associated sound. Then you learned that those sounds were combined to create words. And, then those words could be combined to create sentences, paragraphs, and so on.

In short, much of what you've learned was layered onto things that you already know. And this is true for how you still learn. Your learning is hinged on thoughts, ideas, and information that you already know. This notion of learning is true for everyone.

With that, another way of educating people on how to recognize referrals for you is by tapping into things they already know. You can effectively do this via the use of analogies or metaphors.

An *analogy* is a comparison between two things to show how they are alike in certain ways. The purpose of this to explain or clarify unfamiliar concepts by relating them to familiar ones (e.g., the human brain is like a computer).

A *metaphor*, on the other hand, is a figure of speech that describes one thing by implying a similarity to something else. The purpose is to create vivid imagery by linking them to familiar concepts (e.g., time is a thief).

Analogies and metaphors! The difference is crystal clear, right? No?! It's not to me either.

The difference between the two might not seem crystal clear—and for this purpose, it doesn't need to be. What matters is that analogies and metaphors help people connect your work to something they already understand.

Here are some examples I've encountered while working with businesses and professionals in AmSpirit Business Connections:

- **Attorney (Estate Planning)**: Creating a will with an attorney is like being a navigator on a ship. Just as a navigator charts a course to ensure that a ship gets to its destination safely, I help clients chart a course to ensure that their assets get to where they want them after they pass.

- **Banker**: Do you know how hotels have concierges who cater to the guests' every need? Well, that's my role at the bank ... to get our clients to the rights person to serve their needs ... checking, savings, investments, loans, etc.

- **Financial Advisor**: Do you know how with the game Tetris it's easy in the beginning and then much harder as the block come in faster? That's like investing. When you start, things are simple, slow moving. In time, it becomes more complex, faster moving. As an advisor this is where I add value to those seeking a secure financial future.

- **Financial Advisor**: Do you know how you go to the doctor for a checkup, just to be sure that everything is fine? That's how I work with current and prospective investment clients. We review their situation, hope that it's well positioned, and fix it where it might not be.

- **Home Inspector**: Do you know how people like to test drive a car before they buy it? Well, I help people test drive a home by inspecting every aspect of it before they buy.

- **IT Professional**: Do you know how your car has a 'service engine' light to forewarn you of trouble? One service we have is installing software on your computer to allow us to monitor and be forewarned of issues.

- **Merchant Services Provider**: Do you know how when you use your credit card you accumulate points or miles so you can get all sorts of free stuff? Well, merchants pay for that! And many are looking to minimize that impact. And I have programs that can help businesses do that.

- **Telecommunication Consultant**: Do you know how when you buy that new car, you're amazed by the technology enhancements? Well, I give business owners a similar feeling by getting them a new cloud-based phone system – they get to experience the wonder and feel of new tech.

- **Telecommunication Consultant**: Do you know how the Secretary of State has someone there to translate with important foreign dignitaries? Well, I help businesses by translating with telecom companies, so the business gets the phone and internet service it needs.

And here are a couple examples I've used to describe our work at AmSpirit Business Connections.

1) Do you know how painful it is to pick up the phone and cold call strangers? Well, we have a program where you meet with others who loathe cold calling to refer each other clients.

2) Do you know how when you watch a foreign language film without subtitles you can't follow the story? Well, often businesses are like that foreign language film, and we'll help them message better so their network is able to refer them.

This is the reality, understanding the notion of using figurative language is easy. Coming up with useful ones for your business or profession might not. It takes work.

What you should do, when you have idle time (driving, waiting in traffic, or out for a walk) is ask yourself these questions:

- What's something about how and when I serve clients that might be difficult to understand?

- How can I relate it to some aspect of life that is somewhat universally understood?

If you devote time and thought to these questions, you will come up with analogies and/or metaphors.

Stop Handing Out Rubik's Cubes

There you have it. A half dozen or so thoughts and ideas on how you can educate your network to recognize referral opportunities for you.

Now, let me ask you this. Have you ever solved a Rubrik's Cube? You know, mechanical puzzle with six faces, each covered by nine colored squares? To solve it, you need rotate the faces until all squares on each side of the cube show the same color. Have you ever solved it?

Admittedly, I have not. I've held a few. I've tinkered with each. And every time I set it down, saying to myself, "Forget it. It's not worth the energy."

To solve a Rubrik's Cube takes a ton of critical thinking. And generally speaking, we humans do not like to engage in critical thinking unless we're duly motivated to do.

If you offer me $10,000 to solve a Rubrik's Cube, I will (most people would). There is a solution to the puzzle and there are methodologies to solving it. Moreover, there are tutorials online and books at the library. But short of 5-figure motivation, I'm not going to devote more than a few minutes trying to solve a Rubrik's Cube. And that's the case for most people.

So, here's my point. When you are not crystal clear as to what a good referral for you is, you are essentially handing your network a Rubrik's Cube and saying, "solve this for me."

Chances are they won't. They might not say that. They might smile and nod, leaving you think that they might. But they will quickly move on from what you've asked.

You need to take the time to think through how to create recognition in the minds of your network. Are you following (or running afoul) of the guidelines I've indicated above?

If you want referrals, you need to become artful at creating recognition. Why? Because no one will take the time (nor expend the energy) to figure what you're trying to say.

Think about that. And be honest in answering this: Have you ever devoted more than five minutes trying to figure out what someone else means when they share with you something, like: "Refer me those small businesses you know that want to take a holistic approach to leading their team."

The answer is likely, no. And, if you won't put in the effort for someone else, they likely won't do it for you.

Failure to Empower Engagement

"I was talking to a friend, and she was talking about all her financial concerns, especially getting their kids through college. I recognized that was a perfect opportunity for you. Unfortunately, they didn't ask if I knew a financial advisor. Maybe a referral will happen next time."

I've heard comments like this many times. At Chapter meetings of AmSpirit Business Connections. At Chamber functions. At lunch with small groups of people.

Wait – what? You can have people in your life who know you, like you, and trust you … who are able to spot referral opportunities for you … but you still might not get referrals?

Sadly, it's true. Developing strong relationships and educating your network on how to spot referrals for you is **not enough**.

Why Relationships and Education Aren't Enough

Think about it.

When you get someone to **know** and **like** you, you've touched their heart.

When you get someone to **trust** you, you've triggered a favorable reaction in their gut.

When you educate someone on how to **recognize** referrals for you, you've activated the reticular activation system in their brain.

And those are all great things when it comes to getting a referral. But for person A to refer you to person B, person A needs to say something.

The final reason you might not be getting referrals is that you've failed to empower your network with the ability to talk to others about the value you provide.

A Personal Story

Years ago, while I was still practicing law, there was a member in what is now AmSpirit Business Connections—let's call him Jerry. He was a business psychologist who helped entrepreneurs and professionals overcome self-limiting beliefs and other mental obstacles impacting their businesses.

Jerry was easy to know, like, and trust. He also did a decent job educating us on how to recognize referrals for him. One day, I spotted a referral opportunity for Jerry.

I had a business client who hired me to help her expand her company. But every time we made progress, she would inexplicably pump the brakes. Something was holding her back.

One day, during a visit to her office, I understood the problem. Her ex-husband still worked in the business, parading around with a gun strapped to his hip. Was it loaded? I didn't know—and didn't care to find out. But it was clear that his presence created a toxic, intimidating environment that impacted my client.

My client needed help. And I recognized that Jerry would be a great person to assist her. Except, I didn't know what to say. The situation was sensitive, and I worried about approaching it the wrong way.

Preserving my attorney-client privilege, I met with Jerry and explained the situation. He coached me on how to start the conversation and provided language I could use to discuss the matter with my client.

Following Jerry's advice, I invited my client to lunch. I told her that I considered her not just a good client but a friend. Then— swallowing hard— I said what Jerry instructed me to.

Her eyes teared up. She gently nodded and thanked me for caring. Then she confirmed that I was right.

With that opening, I explained Jerry's expertise and suggested she meet with him for an initial conversation.

Long story short, my client met with Jerry. She then retained him. And within six month's my client's ex-husband was an ex-employee too. And her business lurched forward in a big way.

Not All Referrals Are Sensitive

Some of you might think, "Great story, Frank, but my business doesn't involve sensitive topics like that." I get it. Some industries—such as mental health, weight loss, or life insurance— deal with delicate subject matter. Others, like real estate or accounting, don't.

Even if your product or service isn't sensitive to discuss, you should still approach referrals with nuance. Telling your network to "just tell people to call me—I'm the best" isn't enough.

Yes, there are people in my life who I can refer directly, even bluntly:

> "You need life insurance, dummy. I love you and your family, but I don't want them living with me if something happens to you. So, I'm having Paul call you tomorrow. Don't be a jerk—answer the phone. You're getting a policy, and that's that. Now pass me the nachos."

But if you're counting on your network to refer you like this, you're setting yourself up for failure. Most people aren't comfortable referring others in such a direct way. Instead, most referrals require thoughtful, tactful conversations—like the one I had with my client about Jerry.

Empowering Your Network to Talk About You

Once someone in your network recognizes a referral opportunity for you, they need to say something. If they don't, the referral will never happen—it will remain just a thought stuck in their head.

You can't expect your network to figure out what to say on their own. You know best what your network should say to refer you effectively.

To help, I recommend using a two-part framework to empower your network with language they can use:

Part 1: Initial Engagement: Empower your network with ideas on how to *ease into the conversation* about the referral opportunity.

> For example, with my client, it wouldn't have worked for me to bluntly say, "You need a business psychologist" or "Call Jerry—he'll help you." At worst, I could have offended her; at best, I would have looked foolish. Either way, the referral opportunity would have been lost.
>
> Instead, Jerry helped me transition from small talk to the sensitive topic in a way that felt natural:
>
> > "You know, [Client], we've both been frustrated that [initiative] hasn't reached its potential. When I visited your office the other day, I met your ex-husband and noticed how he conducted himself. I couldn't help but wonder if that might be part of

the problem. I could be wrong—totally wrong—and if I am, I apologize. But I sense an intimidation there, and it might be affecting others in the office, maybe even you."

Notice how I didn't mention Jerry or his services right away. Instead, I transitioned the conversation toward the situation I recognized.

Of course, I took a risk in doing what I did. And, no doubt, there is no guarantee that the conversation would go the way I wanted. My client could have fired me on the spot. My client could have been in denial. My client could have shared additional information that would have demonstrated that I was, in fact, completely wrong.

But I took the risk for two reasons – both compelling to me. One, I liked Jerry and wanted to help him. And two, I cared about my client. And for those reason I went the extra mile.

Now, here's the thing, if you've built a great relationship with your network, they'll be willing to take a similar risk for you (or perhaps your situation is not nearly as touchy as this one). But they will only take the risk, if you've empowered them with language that helps transition a conversation towards a situation you can add value to.

Part 2: Empowered Transition: Teach your network how to connect you with those people in the situation who can benefit from your expertise.

Once your network is successfully conversing with someone in general terms about the referral opportunity (via your empowerment), then you need to teach them how to connect you to the situation.

This requires a little patience. For example, I said what I indicated above, let my client process it, and then let her speak.

From there, we talked. I asked more questions. I wanted to explore and flesh out the situation. I wanted to be sure that Jerry was the right solution. After all, my client could have said any number of these that would have shut the process down.

For example, she might have said, "Yes, I know I have an issue. I've been working with someone, and we're working through it," or "Yes, I know I have an issue. But it's none of your business." Or she might have thanked me for my concern and not wanted to talk any more about it.

Fortunately for Jerry (and my client ... and me), the conversation unfolded in a very positive manner. My client had her moment and then acknowledged that she needed help.

The other benefit of coaching your network to gather some additional information, is that it will allow them to come across as more reflective and with greater creditability. That was certainly my case. When the time was right, I was very comfortable bringing Jerry up in the conversation.

> "You know, I really sorry about all of this. But based that, you might talk with a business psychologist type. Someone that can listen objectively and help you work through how to resolve the situation. If you don't know one, I can help you find someone. In fact, there is someone I'm thinking of right now."

At this point, I brought Jerry's name into the conversation. In so doing, I was reserved in my approach. After all, I was talking about her time, her money, and the direction of her life.

In short, you don't want to encourage your networking to come across as too salesy on your behalf. Think about it. Something like, "you need my consultant friend ... he's the best," is off putting, at best. And you don't want your network to poison a situation with that. So, you want to go with something like:

> "Trust me, you're not alone. There are many others dealing with these sorts of challenges. And Jerry's successfully worked to those people. I think you'll like Jerry, [client]. You don't need to commit to work with him. He's not expecting that. He's the sort that is just hopefully that you'll meet with him and see if there is a level of comfort. Could I introduce you?"

Certainly, at this point, there was a chance that my client could have said no. And there is a chance that the person your networks is talking with could do the same. But done right, it's not likely.

What is likely – as with Jerry and my client – is your network is able to generate a referral for you. That's not a guarantee of business, but it appropriately positions you in the right place at the right time.

Final Thoughts

Strong relationships and education are critical, but they aren't enough. To get referrals, you must empower your network to talk about you. By providing them with clear, tactful ways to engage and transition conversations, you ensure that referral opportunities turn into action.

Crafting Powerful Commercials

"Three birds are perched on a wire. Two decide to fly away. How many are left?"

On the surface, that seems like a simple math problem – three minus two equals one, right? But the answer is actually three.

Why? Because deciding to take action isn't the same as taking action

If you're reading this and thinking, "Yea, I'm going to lean into this," don't stop there. Deciding is meaningless unless you act. And when I say, "take action," it doesn't need to be perfect—it just needs to be action.

As a professor once said in graduate school, "An imperfect plan executed, is always better than the unexecuted perfect plan."

What Action Should You Take?

The answer is simple: craft powerful commercials — messages that do three things:

1) Educates your network on how to **_recognize_** an opportunity for you (and why the situation matters); and,
2) Empowers your network with ideas and insights as to how they can generally **_engage_** with others about that opportunity, and
3) Teaches your network how to **_connect_** you to the person who can benefit from your expertise.

An Example of a Powerful Commercial

Here's a powerful commercial that a real estate agent might use:

1. **Educate them to recognize an opportunity (and why it situation matters):**

    "If you know someone who is getting up in age and living in a two- or three-story home, that could be a good referral for me. As people age, navigating stairs becomes more difficult, and they may be contemplating a move."

2. **Empower them to engage others about the opportunity.**

    "If you know someone in this situation, ask them how they're managing the stairs in their home. Chances are, they'll share their thoughts and concerns."

3. **Teach them how to connect you the person who can benefit:**

    "When they're ready, let them know you have a realtor who can help sell their property quickly at market value and assist them in finding a ranch, patio home, or single-story condo."

An important point to make is that in this powerful commercial, the real estate agent is asking to be referred to older individuals. But that would only be one powerful commercial this professional would ask for ... could ask for ... should ask for.

Don't Only Sell Vanilla

When it comes to crafting powerful messages, approach it as if you operated an ice cream shop. Yes, a store the shares out little scoops of frozen, sugary heaven to boys and girls of all ages.

Now, if you had an ice cream shop, no doubt you'd want it to be the best. The world's best. Super successful, right? To make that happen, would you only serve vanilla?

Of course not. You'd have lots of flavors. Chocolate. Mint. Fudge Swirl. Rocky Road. And you'd change out flavors here and there, like seasonal specials. Essentially, you'd cater to your various customers and their changing tastes. You'd have a little something for everyone.

Now, use that same mindset when you think of how to message for referrals. Don't get stuck with one boring flavor that only a few people have a taste for.

Sure, the vanilla pitch is useful. But there are times when you need something else. A commercial that is like, say, Chocolate. Mint. Fudge Swirl. Rocky Road. Cater to your audience. Have a little something for everyone.

What do I mean by this? Well, I touched on this in the **Failure to Create Recognition** chapter. Continuing using real estate agents as an example. These professionals could literally craft dozens of powerful commercials around the various people that need what they do.

Sure, they help buyers find a home. And they help sellers find a purchaser. But people buy and sell homes lots of different reasons. And they could craft a powerful commercial around each of those different reasons. In fact, I shared four in the **Failure to Create Recognition** chapter.

And the real estate agent could (should) craft a powerful commercial around a few dozen other things. After all, there are many different scenarios where the real estate agent helps people buy or sell real estate. And for each situation, they could craft a powerful commercial.

Here's the thing. If a real estate agent can come up with dozens of messages, then so could you. Whatever you do, clients use you for a variety of reasons.

For example, when I practiced law, no two of my clients were the same. And even the ones who came to me for a similar service (say, to buy or sell a business), each had a nuance to their situation (i.e., different industry, unique twist to the transaction, etc.). And thus, I had a treasure trove of potential messages I could share out.

Avoid the All-Encompassing Message

Someone might ask, "Wouldn't it be better to craft a single commercial that covers everything?"

While this seems logical, it's not practical.

When you try to say everything, you often end up saying nothing.

For instance, as I shared in the **Failure to Create Recognition** chapter, I once used a generic pitch: "I'm Frank Agin, an attorney who provides legal services for the life of your business."
I intended that commercial to say everything. And in my mind, I thought it did. But to my audience, it was vague and unhelpful. A targeted message resonates more effectively.

Consistent Interactions Build Relationships

Another concern might be, "If I share a targeted message for opportunity A, won't I miss out on opportunity B?"

In theory, yes. That is a risk. But here's the thing. If you're meeting someone for the first time, they aren't likely to refer you anyway.

And if you share out something all encompassing (e.g., "Legal services for the life of your business."), it's likely that won't know what you're saying, and you'll miss both opportunity A and B, as well as C through Z.

Remember, before someone gives you a referral, they need to have a relationship with you. And that relationship will not happen in a single encounter. Rather, the notion of a relationship is that there are ongoing interactions.

In a setting like with AmSpirit Business Connections (or similar organizations), people are meeting and interacting with the same people on a periodic basis. And outside of the context of a recurring structured meeting, this is still valid.

For example, when I was practicing law, I would have routine interactions with other professionals (i.e., people I was hopeful of getting referrals from). Phone calls. E-mail exchanges. Scheduled appointments to touch base. Lunch meetings. Running into one another at events.

And whenever we'd connect, they would ask something like, "What's new, Frank?" That's an invitation to share about something different.

> "Thanks for asking. Last week, I helped a business negotiated a lease where I was able to work in for my

client an option to purchase the building at the end of the lease."

Know Your Audience

Someone might ask, "How do I know what to share out? Again, I don't want to message for A, if B is where there is an opportunity."

That's a valid concern. You want to share commercials that make the most sense. What I suggest is that you know your audience and appropriately message from there.

What I mean is that if I were talking with a commercial banker (someone who did lots of lending to businesses buying property), I would likely share about negotiating a purchase option in a lease. If I were talking with an accountant, I might mention how I represented a client before the IRS.

Even when you meet with someone for the first time, you can sneak into your all-encompassing language something specific. For example, when I was out networking as an attorney, I might say:

> "I'm Frank Agin. I'm a business attorney dealing with legal matters for the entire life cycle of a business. For example, last week, I helped a business negotiated a lease where I was able to work in for my client an option to purchase the building at the end of the lease. But that's just one of many things."

So, there is little debate. No matter your business or profession, you should share out different messages here and there. And you should be smart and strategic about what you share when.

Preparation Is Key

But deciding to do that is not enough, right? You need to take action. That is have a series of messages lined up to share.

Now, someone might respond, "Mmmeh, Frank. I'll act on the fly."

Really? You really want to go with that approach? Hmmm? I suggest you think again on that tactic. Why?

Well, I often ask members of AmSpirit Business Connections, "How would you behave if a million dollars were hanging in the balance? How would you conduct yourself, if you knew that later today, you'd be sitting across from bigshot, uber-rich decision maker and you knew that if everything went in your favor, you'd land a deal worth seven figures?

I don't know the exact answer to that question (because I don't know enough about you or your business), but I know that it would not involve shrugging your shoulders and saying, "I'll wing it, baby!"

No! You'd prepare – and prepare in a big way. Right? So, we agree, that if a million dollars were hanging in the balance, you'd put in the work.

Well, here's the thing: A million dollars is (or soon will be) hanging in the balance. It's true. That encounter is coming. It might not happen today. Or tomorrow. Or next week, month, year, or whenever. But that million-dollar moment is coming.

And it may not all be in one deal. It might. That does happen. But it's more likely that it starts with a smaller deal. One that you might consider, "meh." And that small deal then leads to another, and another, and another. Each deal getting bigger and bigger. And when you add it all up, you're looking at a million dollars.

So, looming on the horizon for you, a million dollars is truly hanging in the balance. That's great. You'll take it, right? So, if you'll take it, then why not prepare for it? Logically, if you want more, preparation is key.

Crafting Commercials from Real-World Experiences

When I help people message better about referrals, I find that it's generally effective to get them talking about the clients they're working with. And I don't want them talking in a general sense. Something like, "I work with small businesses who needs help becoming more productive or profitable."

Rather – and this is an actual situation – I insist that they talk about a particular client (on a no-name basis, of course). From that, I will get them to share something definitive. Such as:

> "I'm working with a business owner who wants to load up on inventory or supplies to take advantage of better pricing. The problem is that they having trouble getting traditional bank funding. So, I'm helping them explore non-traditional funding options as well as working with them to create a winning loan package."

This message is somewhat specific. And when they shared it, I immediately started to review my mental Rolodex or CRM for business owner who might be frustrated getting funding to build up inventories or stocking up on supplies.

But that was just one client they were working with. There were others. Each unique. Each gave me a better understanding of how I could recognize a good referral for them. This person thought more, and went on:

"I'm working with this guy who is continually in and out of business. Always trying to launch and re-launch a business ... or different businesses ... and struggling to find any lasting success. I'm helping him get focused on one. Together we're writing a business plan. And I'm going to ensure that is disciplined and consistently executing on it."

"I have a client who has been passed up for promotion twice. She feels unappreciated. But more importantly, she now realizes that she's unfulfilled by the corporate life. So, I'm helping her explore what it would look like to create a business is more aligned with her passion and allows her to unutilized talents."

"I'm working with a newer real estate agent. My parents were realtors and I helped them growing up. So, I know the industry. As a result, I created a program that helps newer with proven tactics and practical strategies that helps then great traction."

When it comes to recognizing referrals for this person, them telling me about clients they were working with is a productive exercise. And it was infinitely more useful than continuing to say, "I work with small businesses who needs help becoming more productive or profitable."

In fact, if this person could easily craft these into powerful 30-second commercials. To do so, they might consider slightly tweaking each of these narratives. Then adding on verbiage that offers ideas on how others could generally engage in conversation about the opportunity. And then adding words to teach others how to connect the person to those who can benefit.

Using AI to Craft Commercials

Another approach to becoming prepared is leveraging artificial intelligence (AI).

Let me illustrate this through real world experience. Recently, I was preparing to present to a Chapter of AmSpirit Business Connections on the notion of "talking in when's." That is, stop telling me *what* you do. Rather, tell me *when* you do it. So, I opened Chat GPT Open AI and prompted it to:

> "Take on the role of a real estate attorney and generate a list of the various sorts of legal services they might perform."

Within a few minutes Chat detailed 30 different situations *when* a real estate attorney serves their clients. So that can be a useful strategy for creating 30-second commercial prompts.

Now, a skeptical someone might challenge as to whether the 30 different situations were realistic. Fair. While I did not intend to prove that out, I wanted to create an exercise to use within AmSpirit Business Connections.

So, I took half the list and created a one-page flyer. And made copies for everyone in a Chapter. I passed the flyer out to the entire membership with the following two-front instructions:

1. For the Chapter's real estate attorney, I asked him to review the list and confirm that, in fact, he could and does do all the things listed.

2. For everyone else, I asked them to circle the items that they did not realize the real estate attorney did.

After a minute or two, I asked the real estate attorney if the list was a fair reflection of the services he provided. He confirmed it was (but, not surprisingly, he also indicated that there were other things not on the list).

Then, I asked the other members how many items they'd circled (i.e., how many that they did not realize the real estate attorney did). Most had circled at least ten items. And each of those items represented situations where a member would have likely not referred the real estate attorney because they were educated enough to recognize a referral opportunity.

Important Final Thoughts

This story makes two important points. First, it shows you a way to act by using technology. Take the prompt I use (which I've repeated below) and insert your business or profession.

> "Take on the role of a [INSERT YOUR BUSINESS OR PROFESSION] and generate a list of the various sorts of legal services they might perform."

Second, my story demonstrates that undertaking this exercise may well result in more referrals for you. Consider the real estate attorney. He now knows that his fellow members were unaware of at least ten different potential referral opportunities for him. And he can create messaging to capitalize on that.

Now transpose that situation on top on yours. Isn't it likely – even just a itty bitty little bit – that there might be a disconnect between when you serve your clients and when your network thinks you do?

This disconnect represents potential referrals that turn into clients, invoices, and eventually payments to you. So, if you're one of those birds sitting on that wire, it's time to actually take flight.

Is This for Me?

"That Frank! He's full of it!"

Yes, it's true – I am full of it. But not on this. Not at all.

There are three reasons – and only three reasons – you don't get referrals. I've laid it out as best I can.

1. **Create relationships** so your network knows, likes, and trusts you.
2. **Educate your network** on how to recognize opportunities for you.
3. **Empower your network** with ideas on how to engage others about those opportunities and connect you with the person who can benefit from your expertise.

It's that simple.

But does this mean that anyone who reads this will fall in line and suddenly be blessed with endless referrals?

No! Of course, not. Life is not that simple. There are formulas, but the key to any formula is having the discipline to follow it.

The Discipline to Follow the Formula

Think about it.

The formula for financial well-being has been known for millennia. Financial planning became formalized during the Renaissance, and the Industrial Revolution brought forth savings and investment institutions. Modern figures like Suze Orman and Dave Ramsey have produced countless books, programs, and courses on the topic.

Yet, financial illiteracy still plagues society.

Similarly, the formula for weight loss – the balance of calories and energy – has been understood since the mid-1800s. By the 1950s, the fitness boom, driven by pioneers like Jack LaLanne, brought the message to the masses. Since then, books, articles, programs, and retreats on weight loss have proliferated.

And yet stretchy pants are more popular than ever.

So, I know – sadly – that this book will change nothing for many. They'll read it, say it's great, and decide to act. But like those two birds who decided to fly away, they'll remain perched in their old ways.

Why I Wrote This Book

If I know most people won't truly act on what's in this book, why did I write it?

I wrote it for one person: Jim Alavi.

Jim's Story

The concepts in this book I talk about incessantly within AmSpirit Business Connections. A few years ago, I was preparing to talk at an AmSpirit event when Jim Alavi came up to me, shook my hand, and laughed, "So, Frank. What are you talking about today?"

I knew his question was rhetorical, but I answered anyway; "Jim, I'm giving the same presentation I gave at your Chapter three weeks ago. And the same one you saw me give at the Chapter you visited last week."

Jim laughed and replied, "You know, when I heard you give this presentation the first time, I thought, '*That Frank! He is full of it!*'"

Hearing that stung. I'm passionate about what I do, and no one likes to feel dismissed.

But Jim wasn't finished. "But the second time I heard it," he said, "I thought, 'Why not just try doing what Frank is saying?' So, I did."

Jim's Results

Jim's original weekly commercial was something like this:

"I'm Jim Alavi, a home inspector with K&J Inspections. A good referral for me is anyone who needs a home inspection."

But after hearing my advice, he made a key change:

"If you know someone buying a rural property outside the city limits, that could be a good referral for me. Most rural homes have septic systems, which require a special inspection. I'm certified to do those. Refer them to me, and I can inspect both the home and the septic system."

Jim also included language to help his network engage with rural property owners and taught them how to connect him with prospects.

It wasn't perfect, but it was a huge step in the right direction. So, I told him, "Jim, I remember that. I thought it was good."

The results?

He then excitedly shared, "What you don't know, Frank, is that after the meeting, the Chapter attorney came up with me with a referral. She was helping to settle an estate in Hocking County and there was a house and septic system to inspect."

"Great," I responded. I love when members of AmSpirit Business Connections meet with success. But I had to ask, "Well, are you doing the job?" After all, Hocking County is about 75 miles southeast of Columbus.

With a gleam in his eyes, he replied, "No, Frank. I'm not going. I already went. And here's the thing: it wasn't just a house and septic. There were two houses and two septic systems, and a pole barn."

Jim then explained the significance:

"Frank, when I do an average inspection in Columbus, I generate about $X in fees. With this, I earned me nearly $4X."

From that point forward, Jim became a believer. He consistently put in the work, crafting and sharing well-constructed commercials. Now, his network—inside and outside AmSpirit—knows how to recognize opportunities for him and what to say when they encounter one.

His network inside and outside AmSpirit Business Connections know how to recognize opportunities for him and what to say when they encounter one.

The Next Jim Alavi

So no, I didn't write this book for *that* Jim Alavi. I wrote it for the *next* Jim Alavi—the person who says:

> "Why not just try doing what Frank has laid out in this book? What have I got to lose?"

This book isn't for people who won't buy it, won't read it, or won't act on it. It's for the small percentage of elite individuals who:

- Want to become really good at asking for referrals; and,
- Are willing to take action to achieve that goal.

If that's you, then this book is for you.

We Like Referrals, Too

"A good referral for me is ..."

Yes, just like you, I'm in business – owning and operating AmSpirit Business Connections. While I'm skilled at helping others position themselves for referrals, I also rely on referrals. They're the lifeblood of AmSpirit Business Connections, both within the organization and beyond.

Below, I've outlined a few specific referral requests, structured to follow the guidelines I recommend for asking for referrals.

Request #1 ... Looking for A Referral Group

If you know a business professional—such as a real estate agent, mortgage lender, financial advisor, or insurance agent—who is struggling to find a referral group, they could be a great referral for me. These categories often face challenges because their slots in many groups are already filled.

If you know someone in this situation, ask how much they've explored other group options. Give them a chance to share their experience—chances are they haven't spent much time exploring alternatives and may be focused on one or two major groups in their area.

Regardless of their level of research, ask if they're familiar with AmSpirit Business Connections, and encourage them to learn more.

Even better, ask if you can introduce them to me. You can easily do this by email and include me on the message thread (frankagin@amspirit.com). This would allow us to set up a time to talk, get acquainted, and explore how

AmSpirit Business Connections might help them. We could also discuss the possibility of starting an AmSpirit Business Connections chapter in their area.

Request #2 ... Wants A Better Referral Group Experience

If you know someone participating in a networking group who is unhappy with the referrals they're receiving, they could be a good referral for me. Networking groups work differently for everyone, and we strive to identify and address these factors when building chapters of AmSpirit Business Connections.

If you know someone in this situation, ask how much they've explored other group options. Let them share their perspective—chances are they haven't done much, as they've likely been focused on trying to make their current group work.

Regardless of their experience, ask if they're familiar with AmSpirit Business Connections and encourage them to learn more.

Even better, ask if you can introduce them to me. You can easily do this by email and include me on the message thread (frankagin@amspirit.com). We could set up a time to talk. From there, we could get acquainted, I could share more about AmSpirit Business Connections, and we could discuss the possibility of starting an AmSpirit Business Connections chapter and how we address referral challenges head-on.

Request #3 ... Seeking More Support for Their Referral Group

If you know of a group participating in a networking organization that feels underserved, that could be a great opportunity for me. Like any business, some organizations inadvertently overlook or fail to fully support certain groups.

If you're in contact with someone associated with an underserved group, ask how much they've explored support from other organizations. Give them space to share their answer—chances are they've done some initial exploration but nothing in-depth.

Regardless of where they are in the process, ask if they're familiar with AmSpirit Business Connections, and encourage them to learn more.

Even better, ask if you can introduce them to me. You can easily do this by email and include me on the message thread (frankagin@amspirit.com). We could set up a time to talk. From there, we could get acquainted, and I could share more about AmSpirit Business Connections. We could also discuss the possibility of converting their group into a chapter of AmSpirit Business Connections and how we'd ensure they are fully supported and satisfied.

Request #4 ... Professional Looking to Improve Their Ability To Get Referrals

A good referral for me would be an introduction to an entrepreneurial-minded professional—perhaps a coach or consultant—who's actively looking to build a clientele. These professionals place a high value on being well-networked and might be interested not only in joining a chapter of AmSpirit Business Connections but also in helping us lead and grow the organization.

If such a person comes to mind, ask what they're doing to get better networked and generate referrals. Give them space to share their answer—they will likely have much to share.

Regardless of their response, suggest that they explore learning about AmSpirit Business Connections, as we have a program where they can be compensated for building a referral network.

Even better, ask if you can introduce them to me. You can easily do this by email and include me on the message thread (frankagin@amspirit.com). We could set up a time to talk. From there, we could get acquainted, and I could share more about AmSpirit Business Connections and opportunities within the organization.

Request #5 … Planner Seeking Program on Referrals

If you know an event planner or an individual tasked with organizing a conference—perhaps for an HR, financial services, or real estate improvement—they could be a good referral for me. In addition to running AmSpirit Business Connections, conferences hire me to deliver professional development programs on the science of relationships and underutilized aspects of business networking.

If you know such a person, when the time is right, ask to what extent professional relationships and business networking are important in their industry. Chances are, that will evoke a positive response.

If it does, suggest that they consider bringing me into their programming. Even better, ask if you can introduce them to me. You can easily do this by email and include me on the message thread (frankagin@amspirit.com). We could set up a time to talk. From there, we could get acquainted, and I could share more about the various programs I deliver and how they would add value to their conference or event.

Request #6 … Sales Team Seeking Referral Best Practices

If you know the leaders of a sales team or division — perhaps a sales manager, territory leader, or sales VP — they could be a good referral for me. In addition to running AmSpirit Business Connections, companies that rely on a human sales force often have me work with their reps on best practices for networking and generating referrals.

If you know such a sales leader, ask to what extent they stress business networking and referrals. Chances are, they'll share that it's important but that many of their reps are underperforming in those areas.

Whatever the case, suggest that they consider talking with me about empowering their sales reps with ideas and tools for networking smarter and achieving better results. Even better, ask if you can introduce them to me. You can easily do this by email and include me on the message thread (frankagin@amspirit.com). We could set up a time to talk. From there, we could get acquainted, and I could share more about the various programs I deliver and how they could add value to their team.

Thank you for taking the time to review this. We truly appreciate any and all introductions, as they could lead to great referrals. Even if AmSpirit Business Connections isn't the right fit for them, something positive could still come from the connection.

As Brian Miller shares in his book Three New People: "You have no idea what kind of opportunities await you just on the other side of the next connection."

Request #7 ... Podcast Host Seeking a Guest

If you know someone with a podcast that focuses on business, entrepreneurship, or corporate human resources, they might be a good referral for me. Podcasters are often looking for guests to interview, and I have extensive content and experience, having appeared on more than 100 different podcasts.

If you know someone who hosts a podcast like this, simply ask if they're looking for guests. If they are, ask if you could introduce them to me—someone with a strong background in professional relationships and business networking. As a start, I could share a PDF that provides an overview of the topics I can discuss and the value I could bring to their audience.

Request #8 ... Business Professional Seeking Development

If you know a business professional who shares or shows an interest in their personal or professional development, they could be a good opportunity for me. I'm the author of several books that can help them build a stronger network and generate more referrals.

If you know someone like this, ask if they have an interest in topics related to professional relationships, business networking, or best practices for generating referrals. If they seem interested, suggest they look into my work.

Many of my books are available on Amazon and other platforms in print, electronic, and audio formats. They can view them all at frankagin.com.

About The Author

Frank Agin is the founder and president of AmSpirit Business Connections, which empowers entrepreneurs, sales representatives, and professionals to become successful and get more referrals through networking.

He also shares information and insights on professional relationships, business networking, and best practices for generating referrals on his Networking Rx podcast and through various professional programs.

Finally, Frank is the author of several books, including *Foundational Networking: Building Know, Like & Trust to Create a Lifetime of Extraordinary Success*. See all his books and programs at www.frankagin.com.

You can contact him at frankagin@amspirit.com.